The Future

Also by Monica Ferrell

The Answer Is Always Yes
Beasts for the Chase
You Darling Thing

The Future

MONICA FERRELL

Four Way Books
Tribeca

Library of Congress Cataloging-in-Publication Data

Names: Ferrell, Monica author
Title: The future / Monica Ferrell.
Description: Tribeca : Four Way Books, 2026.
Identifiers: LCCN 2025027285 (print) | LCCN 2025027286 (ebook) | ISBN 9781961897823 trade paperback | ISBN 9781961897830 ebook
Subjects: LCGFT: Poetry
Classification: LCC PS3606.E7535 F88 2026 (print) | LCC PS3606.E7535 (ebook) | DDC 811/.6--dc23/eng/20250625
LC record available at https://lccn.loc.gov/2025027285
LC ebook record available at https://lccn.loc.gov/2025027286

This book is manufactured in the United States of America and printed on acid-free paper.

Four Way Books is a not-for-profit literary press. We are grateful for the assistance we receive from individual donors, public arts agencies, and private foundations including the New York State Council on the Arts, a state agency.

We are a proud member of the Community of Literary Magazines and Presses.

CONTENTS

I Appreciate Your Visibility 3
Plastikos 5
The Fifties 7
Subclinical 9
Don't Be a Baby 11
If Only, If Only 13
Lepanto 15
Winter Song 17
The Slow Parade 18
With Amulets 20
Duino Elegies 22
You Can Fold Me 29
Box of Sighs 31
Ultrasonogram 33
Hôtel du Palais 34
In Safranbolu 35
I Have Lost It 37
Lucky Girl 39
The Labor Hours 41
Infancy 43
Life of Mary 44
Calling the Name 50
Plans for the Next Ice Age 52
At the Stop & Shop 54
Provision 56
Giambattista Vico 58
Wearing the Purple 59
Siren 61
Private Property 63
Killing Moths 65
A Day in March 67
Small Talk About Weather 68
L'Hallali 70

The Eighteenth Century 71
Twelve Variations on Etchings by Goya 72
Andromeda 75
The Book of Judith 77
What a Surprise 78
The Spanish Flu 80
The Wake 81
Angkor Wat 82
Little Voice 83
Is It All Right 84
Cosmos 86
Fossil 87
Childhood 88
At the Price Chopper 89
I Have Found It 94

Notes

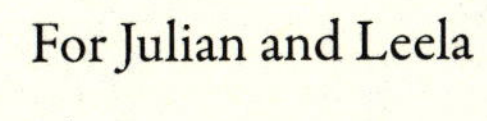
For Julian and Leela

"...the future's light never ceases, for even an instant, to wound us..."

—Pier Paolo Pasolini

I APPRECIATE YOUR VISIBILITY

Every day I wake up
And ask is it today?
The volcano?

People say Monica,
Monica, you live in Vermont:
There are no volcanos.

Oh but this one,
It's on the horizon,
Bunched, a black horse,

Saddlebags spilling over
Ropes of glowing red,
Each day inching closer—

On the customer helpline,
The bot inside the machine
Who's been chatting with me

A good fifteen minutes
Asks if he's resolved my quest;
I type yes, yes you have.

He thanks me. Tells me he
Appreciates my visibility.
The only thing lit in this room is my screen.

PLASTIKOS

I'm made of plastic:
Plastic eyes,
Plastic throat,

Plastic ovaries, their little seeds
Lined up like the diminutive
Winged unicorns and swings

Of my girl's Polly Pocket
Purse: plastic
Fever and dream.

Plastic sex.
In marine depths, the flapjack
Octopus and bloodybelly

Comb jelly shiver
At the sweet
Touch of polyamorous

Polyethylene;
In Alpine meadows, plastic edelweiss
Squints at a sky

Where the sun wonders what

The hell's gotten

Into everyone

THE FIFTIES

They were such innocents
They took straight razors to clean faces
Smoked and drank milk at the same time
Crammed whole junkyards with steel

Nearly never touched plastic
Whatever they touched was real
The TV was a box of shadows
In the living room

And if you wanted really to go crazy
There was always the bomb shelter
They were babies, comparatively
They woke each day completely new

They never had to worry about memories
Swelling and following them like algal blooms
Through the internet's tides of forever—
I don't even know what starch is

And have never used Brylcreem
Or testified, sweating liberally,
Before the Un-American Committee
I'll bet back then was crummy too

With the same fevers and pus
Though they probably let you die of colon cancer
Without making you defecate first
Into a box lab techs will scan for polyps

And if you looked nothing at all like me
They probably left you alone at the lunch counter
With *Meditations in an Emergency* by O'Hara
The cook in his white apron nods gravely
Both of you know it's serious

SUBCLINICAL

I walk the world with a locked box
Lodged in my chest. Doctor, it hurts
But not as much as it should. In Bucha,

On the roadway of the Street of Apples
A woman lay four weeks straight
Unburied even by snow. They saw her red

Coat and rolled right over, Russians,
Tanked and vigilant in their to and fro.
Doctor, there's nothing wrong with me

That isn't also true of many others.
At night I sleep under a vast epiphany
That hasn't descended upon me,

Pinpricks that shine a white writing
I can't read. I don't want to know
Yet. Instead I ask to stay here, greedy

For the smell of autumn. Before
Leaving, I've made a miniature of me
To witness the raising of the sea,

To watch over the unimaginable,
To greet this revelation of a future
With those new names it will need.

DON'T BE A BABY

Baby,
Stop crying.
There's only so many

Tears in this world,
You're keeping factories
Occupied, workers

On the clock who need
To focus on bullets—
Haven't you heard?

Yes, for the front lines;
Now everywhere's a front line.
Bullets, ring lights,

Ozempic, smart tires
And cake-decorator tips
For piping icing

Over this pitted parking
Lot of a planet,
TikTok filters for faces

Who gravely need them,
And start-up equipment
For those ax-throwing

Clubs grown so popular
In Midwestern cities...
Baby, if you won't

Stop wasting tears
Maybe you won't mind
If I take one—

Lightly, saltily—
On my tongue's
Tip.

IF ONLY, IF ONLY

I could put the baby to sleep
Remember my dream

Feed the lion
Be the lion

If only.
I've only been a girl

Who pushed out two or three tots
Then learned to bake

In a house I'm always cleaning
On my knees.

Yet I was born to be
Alexander

In Babylon, or at the very least
A Spanish gentleman

Wearing white slacks
Sometime in the 1970s, who smokes

Dispassionately beneath a streetlamp.
If only

I'd learned to dive
For pearls, breed sheep,

Sing canticles in a boys' choir
Sweetly at Viennese dawn

Here on Earth, just as
I do all these and more

On the moon

LEPANTO

Today I am reading about Occhiali,
born Giovanni Donigi Galeni, an Italian
from Calabria, stolen, enslaved
in an Ottoman galley, an oarsman:
he rowed the soldiers to all the good
battles, Preveza, Djerba, and the Siege of Tripoli,
by then a corsair with his own brigantine;
eventually he fled his janissaries' mutiny
and led a flank at Lepanto, where the admiral
Müezzinzade Ali Pasha was defeated, soundly.
He handed the banner of the Knights of Malta
over to Selim the Second, but what did it matter
when the Banner of the Caliphs was lost?
An enormous green cloth on which verses
from the Koran and Allah's name,
28,900 times, in golden letters, were emblazoned.
I'd like to write something 10,000 times and mean it.
It's Wednesday, the 23rd November of a millennium.
Somewhere in the history books,
the 400 ships are still burning
on a trash-spattered ocean, Ali Pasha's head
watches the whole scene from the pike
where they placed it in the bow of his own ship.
And Occhiali, Uluj Ali, called by Selim

Kılıç, which means *Sword*, sleeps
peacefully in the mosque he built at the heart
of Istanbul, dreaming in Italian, maybe.
I am still burning within myself, which is
to say, I am alive. I am still working
with the gold thread of the mind's thought
against the banner of the computer's screen,
which always shows me its blank face,
its face of radiant snow, like a graveyard
on which the flakes have fallen thick
enough to bury almost everything
except the few letters here and there
etched on a few dark stones.

WINTER SONG

White edges the branches of the morning tree.
White crisscrosses the open grave,
This unmarked field. At its border,
A cicatrix of tracks heads toward eternity.
The tracks lead elsewhere. Trains
Insert an urgency when they will.
The sleeping grapes, the dead tomatoes:
This was summer, once. I prefer
It now. Prefer silence, marble, the frosted
Cake changed to stone. Prefer blue light
To gold. Not the bare brown trees,
But fitted out in white finery
They make a new kind of heaven—bleached,
Barren, beautiful as the blanked page.

THE SLOW PARADE

Hundreds of thousands of years
On the march,
Fiddling with the bone

Arrowhead and awl,
Devising how to build a wall
Out of the clay of a graveyard,

Inventing flutes and paint,
The first child's name—then they slipped
Out of view, as if off a cliff.

Tonight, over my backyard,
The same old show unrolls, a sky
Of astral axels and triple-lutzes.

Perhaps there's some other sort of star
Back there, balled-up, black,
Whose light is the light of dark matter.

Perhaps it can brighten the banquet
Hall of Neanderthals,
For surely there must be somewhere

They're feasting beneath torches
Made of curved horns from aurochs
That slipped this way before us

Into the long grass and were lost.

WITH AMULETS

When you go out
Wear amulets:
Oh, I don't mean what
You are thinking,

Rabbits' feet, that sort of thing;
I mean your own
Teeth, your own words.
You won't need symbols,

You'll have your memories
Of the worst that's happened,
The first shock. That works better than
Any old blue eye in a palm

Or ring of garlic would.
I'm telling you, you need amulets.
There are bad actors everywhere,
Haven't you seen

Red hats, weird flags
Emblazoned with snakes and runes
All over the parking lot
At the grocery—

So much hocus-pocus,
So much huffing and puffery.
In the Stone Age, they carved
Lines into amber beads

To wear around the neck
And pelvis. As for me?
Can't you see
I have this poetry

DUINO ELEGIES

1.

No one hears. The doll has a mouth and eyes,
has a tongue, has a hand that writes. Yet the small
soul can't reach the surface and goes unknown.
Still, it corresponds. To the knots in the trees,
the throb of blue-white that is a sea
down below, at the bottom of these cliffs
that promise infinity is near—a twist
of the ankle, and it will rush up to you.
The cliffs themselves are solidified shells
piled in their millions from the shallow sea
that once pulsed here too, where I am standing.
Is it wrong to find their scars beautiful?
There is no true state—beyond change, that is.
Ice covered this place once and will return.

2.

As soon as. After. The minute. On one
occasion; previously. Then. Some time
ago. Immediately. The instant.
It was the Pleistocene. The Permian.

The Hadean—why? Because everywhere
was burning. What stood here, where I am
was orange and hot like you can't believe.
Forget the polar bears: the only thing
that lived then was nothing, which is a kind
of life the way zero is a number.
Taking the long view. Eventually. At
the end of the day. How soon is now?
I've never been at home in a second;
an hour is the white chalked round a corpse.

3.

They invented caves. Castles and woodwinds.
The kouros. Sharp staves, cylinder seals.
Invented the eighteenth century, music
boxes and public fountains. We could go
at this all day, naming. What surprises me
is that the girl, when she leaves my body,
starts blank as a cloudbank taping shut the sky.
I begin by giving her all the names I know.
I fill her up with them in the milk I give
until I run out: but it's all right by then.

She'll take it from here, she with all those
other meteors who keep hailing to Earth,
they'll invent new ones, a whole tomorrow
hammered out of names I haven't heard.

4.

No one's lived in this place a hundred years.
Most days, the mirrors are empty but for light,
the face of a bare wall opposite. Here
something ceased being—a way of life,
princesses, the carronade. Candlelight.
But how can anyone ever vanish?
Think of a painting: the hours transferred
into the canvas by that artist standing
at easel, dwelling in it. Those hours stay
and reverberate; they enter me, the viewer,
through the colors' frequency till suddenly
this evening has a strange sweetness...
like an ancient ammonite changed utterly
to iridescent ammolite: everything rainbow.

5.

I lived with a man with a cat who was dying.
Well, before it died, it disappeared.
Two days, I couldn't find it. Then at last
it comes stalking out from his room
like a revenant from the grave, straight
to me—swear to God—tears in its eyes,
like *Not one day more, please.* That was it.
Such dignity. We called the taxi,
a vet saw us right away. On the table,
the cat looked only at me, like a last light
fading. And that's it—right? Right?
In my daughter's science book
are pictures, questions. *Is a tree alive? A pen?
A mountain?* In all honesty, I know nothing.

6.

To unremember everything. To unpack
the body of all its references. And who
are the handmaidens of this operation?
The boiled soul become gas, all

the ribbons of the flesh's pillows
untied. And in the soil then to give up
nitrogen, manganese, cobalt for some
other animal's use. The eyes dissolve
their own visions, as dirt dissolves the eyes.
Only a whiff of dream remains
above the scene of the splayed calcium,
an architecture left behind like the broken
walls of Troy. To unbecome, walk backward
into twilight that turns toward a different dawn.

7.

Imagine: ice over Iceland. Over Svalbard,
Franz Josef Land, Novaya Zemlya, the Barents
Sea, which then was not a sea as it didn't move.
And over this strange frozen world, which
from space must have looked extra bluish then,
only a few thousand in our meager herd,
*Homo whatever*s holed up in limestone dwellings,
awaiting the age when our kind would build
a ship that took us to see the view from the moon.
That's a fallacy, though. It isn't waiting

when you don't know what's coming, just as
we've no idea now what's next for us.
Can't ask the citizens of Atlantis how it felt
when the water started whispering, at first a trickle.

8.

I pile alphabet block on alphabet block:
the way the walls in Duino Castle stand
is how I built these embankments for you
to walk upon with a view of churning blue.
Out of letters I grow a courtyard garden
and invite the bees, hoping they will visit
then leave me. Out of lines I weave warp
and weft or woof, a fourteen-stranded fabric,
into my own chronicling tapestry,
where I'll appear poorly proportioned and pale
like the conquerors in the one at Bayeux. Nevertheless,
you have seen me. These two worn brown hands wrote
my bit of backlit graffiti upon a laptop.
Every word of writing is a form of goodbye.

9.

On the one hand, cold, wind, crystals,
the pure abstraction of the subtraction
symbol—bleach, vinegar, the force of waves,
everything that strips away. On the other,
music, night-blooming jasmine, bats and worms,
milk, jade, the color fuchsia, the letter *x*
not as the sign of multiplying but for how
it declares *here, now*. Tattoos. Of course,
that famous smell of babies, hug even of
a stuffed toy penguin, all our animal
verves and instincts, tingle in the dark,
sense of direction. The glass half full,
half empty. I reached between my legs to feel
a soft head. That was you, future, breaking through.

YOU CAN FOLD ME

I don't take up much space
On the airplane

I cross my legs
In bed

I curl into a whorl
In the shower

I bow my head
But what's going on

Inside my brain
Keeps exploding

Full supernova
Getting huger

Every year
That I shrink

It's very deceptive
It's a kind of protection

Sometimes people even
Look through me

Like at that voting booth
In Brooklyn, the man all

Sorry ma'am, didn't see you there
With your screaming children

I said
Fuck you

I invented the future
What the hell is it

You do you think
You're so big?

BOX OF SIGHS

Admit it, admit it
I'm magic,
I make the bells ring,

I sift
The living from the dead,
Acid from salt,

I sit at the hinge, on a
Rocking chair
Dissolving

Into sand, spilling
Hours each night
I wait for sleep

To blow the baby up
Like a balloon
In the Macy's parade.

There are others:
Below the belly
Button in my cave

Of faces stuck
To the flesh's
Red pincushion,

A pomegranate
Uncut.
It's bloody down there.

I don't let them out
Though they'd do
Anything

To take the air,
For a walk on the moon,
Just one sigh.

ULTRASONOGRAM

Invisible seamstresses busy themselves:
with flickering electricity, they stitch
white outlines on a screen of black velvet,
two kidneys, a liver, lungs, and a heart.

Then there's a place for dreaming, the brain
where an unknown scribe has taken up residence,
seated herself before that grand desk
where she'll spend years illuminating scenes.

Events not yet begun. For now, she must be patient
laying out paint and inkpot, vellum pages,
while lab techs bustle as if taking measures
for a bridal gown in millimeters—

preparing for marriage to life, that is:
divorce first from me. Wavering, radiant
white on black, the baby looks awesome
as a Milky Way, and about as distant.

HÔTEL DU PALAIS

Somebody took a wind-up clock
And lobbed it into the Milky Way:

Nobody knows what time
It is or when the damn thing's

Going to ring—
While we're here, though,

The accommodations are very spacious,
I must say, also shining

The view of this excellent canopy cannot be beat
And one feels at home

I'm quite comfortable
In this flesh-toned bodysuit

Would not want to take it off, ever
Would not want to leave

Particularly (it's so awkward) when
I don't know the next destination

IN SAFRANBOLU

The evening I left, I went for a wash
In the neighborhood hammam. Lifted my dress.
Entered the water, which moved in rings
From me as though from a stranger, took a stick
To strip a layer of my old back.
In my bag lay a box of Turkish Delight
Meant for my parents, a book of notes, a passport,
But I was holding nothing now as I floated
In pools upon pools of ancient tiled rooms.
There was a pigeon in an alcove making song,
Women in the shadows clucking disapprovingly
At me, unmarried and brazen
And free, in the windows a kind of violet smoke
I understood as twilight taking over the sky.
However hard I tried to erase the blot
My body kept bobbing back up.
I thought that's what time was, you couldn't lose it
Like a stone in water, that having been
Myself so long it would be forever.
And now Safranbolu doesn't exist anymore,
At least not the one where my father
Still has years on the clock,
Where my mother's unreason hasn't begun,
The babies not sprung yet from their wherever,

City rich off spice, flame-colored threads of the crocus
That flowers on the hills around like blue light,
Whose gates I will pass through only in the mind:
When I slipped on my dress and reopened the door
Night had closed over the world that I knew.

I HAVE LOST IT

It's gone missing, that old notecard
With something crude written
By a man once in a summer
I remember as terribly hot: I read it

Reclined outside in the park
Paging through this huge volume
He'd sent by special messenger
To my address. Wet

As an oasis with afternoon sweat,
I felt voluptuous and infinite
Covered in lines of smutty poetry
That warbled of killing deer,

Diamonds, and the Shah of Iran.
My body was dotted with glue
Upon which petals of oleander
Had fallen and fluttered poisonously there.

Then the sky above the park curled
Into a fist, grew dark: I hailed a cab
And rode through claps of fizzy thunder
Amid a downpour to his crooked little door.

His pajamas were damp.
We drank gin until we didn't.
Next morning, in the dregs at the bottom
Of my glass, I saw a bloated ant:

Its black, round blobs appeared relaxed,
Loosened somehow. *Well,* said the man,
I guess she found what she was looking for.
And because he wasn't exactly wrong,

I forgot the door, forgot the buzzer.
I slipped the card back in its book
Though every now and then I took
It out to sniff for a scent.

LUCKY GIRL

The whims of weather spread white
Over the long meadow toward world's end,
Blotting out any possibility but this one
December dawn with the babies in their cribs
Sleeping as though they always intended

To get here, though I know it could've
Gone another way. We can't ever guess
What time will make of us. Call it
A trick of the wind, barometric pressure,
Luck: it was given to me to watch

This horror movie in the mirror, the one
Where my body morphs to a dun blunder,
Willowy tallow taper unspooling loops
Downed with light brown hair,
As Eliot put it in a poem I once knew

By heart. I was a sixteen-year-old virgin
Then, recording it for the boys to hear
From the taut, unyielding box of
My answering machine. *A naked woman my age*
Is just a total nightmare, wrote Fred Seidel

From his bower on Central Park.
So goes the verdict pronounced by high art.
So goes the view as glimpsed by some few men.
In this life I've fractured and scarred;
Cicatrixed, I waxed, became again thin

And cut other people like a daisy
Chain out of my own skin.
Today I am luckier than aurochs,
Luckier than that cicada in the basement.
I live.

THE LABOR HOURS

A bright-flashing knife splits silk by the bolt—
Everything in this room is metal or meat,

I mean these instruments and machines
Which beep to measure not me but that other

No one's seen yet, whose heart's aflutter,
The organ of some fickle god. I'm not myself,

Am mercury beginning to boil,
Overheating, deforming like the asphalt of July,

I bubble, am undone.
I start out on the ladder's lowest rung and climb.

I lung it through hours of rowing, pulling hard
Across a lake of breaths they say will lead to morning,

It's a heavy lift.
Now would be a good time to cry out,

To shake something until it breaks: these windows
Maybe, night-smeared, plush as wolf-pelts

Torn only where the sun's hot bullet drains life
From a hole. Yes, we did it. It's dawn. We're finished.

I've become a doorway, that threshold step passed
Over when the future clambers out into the open.

INFANCY

The gear in this jaw does nothing.
The muscle in her tongue unlooses only
Raw noise, but the machinery hasn't broken;
It's never been used. The baby doesn't even
Know yet how to sit. She just lies there,
Folded in herself, a scroll whose sutra is written
With still-invisible ink, portent no one can read
About some portion of sun I'll never see.
—But who smithed you, baby?
Who sewed this skin and found your name?
Who labored in dirt till it took the shape of a word?
Who walked the whole way to the orchard's end tree
And shook till you dropped to the earth?
I was the one who blew the trumpet when you came.

LIFE OF MARY

1. *Meeting at the Golden Gate*

What begins: everything. Size of a crumb,
indiscriminate bundle of cells. It's
a barnacle with a dream inside. Cloud
in-sewn with seed pearls. Radiant shape
that in theory she's always carried, but
now she's alone with it—like being alone
with an ocean at night. In the brick arch,
Anne's a second portal, whispering: her
husband listens as though he hasn't grown
suddenly remote as those blue mountains
compared to the future that lies glittering
and inexorable within her. The fact is,
soon, what she'll be is chaff, a passing breeze
through summer leaves: a mother.

2. *Nativity of Mary*

How white these cloths are, clear the water
in its copper basin, white the sheets
and swaddles, as though she has not just lost
a universe of blood: out of which she's made

this golem, a baby girl. The maids look thrilled,
small-breasted, narrow-waisted to a degree
she will not again take as her shape.
Everyone looks happy—even the baby,
casting her mother a tender backward glance
like *So long, farewell*—except for Anne,
dazed, who stares up at the ceiling, searching
its surface perhaps for a door. She never
could've imagined. It's shock, it must be,
this feeling: how she never will forgive them.

3. *Presentation of Mary*

The girl can walk now. She can dress herself
blue: sky-blue, a celestial creature, gift
from God whom they're returning like a parcel
mailed to the wrong address. It's been four years;
Joachim's hair has lost its color, he's old,
he's human, which means the gold is in the sky,
in the temple, around his wife's head
but not for him. He was the one
who starved in the desert till angels came—
nevertheless, no halo. His part is finished.

His hands: is he wringing them? Praying?
Anne looks relieved, simply waves
as Mary slips river-like toward infinity
and dogs play on: theirs is the real heaven.

4. *Marriage of the Virgin*

No one smiles in these scenes, claps or laughs;
some look curious, some side-eye the bride.
Joseph appears ancient, defeated. Mary stares
as the priest's hand covers theirs. She's laid
her other one on the belly half-hidden under
a golden fold. It's a bump shot, this canvas,
glimpse of a secret distending the world,
blowing out air into her body's glass
to the dimensions of its changing shape.
Here you can worship what is so new
it hasn't even arrived, like a slang word
still dreaming in some kid's tongue, unspoken.
Like standing seaside, watching the path of a ship
not yet built, its timber still trees in the forest.

5. *Annunciation*

Angels, a dove, even God—it takes
a village, apparently, to give this news.
And what a mess he's made, that one
who came in, his wings flipping cushions,
scattering lilies' leaves all over the floor.
She was at home, at her ease, she'd kicked
her sandals off, those pretty narrow shoes
that soon won't fit, she was reading a book,
stealing a beat from time's relentless merge
of the one and the many streaming together
toward forever. She doesn't want to stop,
either: see how one hand remains upon
the page ardently, as though, laid there,
it might drink the words out from the paper.

6. *Visitation*

You are blessed, blessed, Elizabeth says;
the truth is they're both mothers of death.
One son will be taken up the hill of spikes,
the other's head will sigh from a platter.

Kids are sailboats you let go, boats folded
from old newspaper, listing in the wind
over the town pond till they sink out of view.
All of us mothers mother death.
The afternoon is infinite on the edge of a field
where bees hum a canticle, intimate
go-between of stamens and anthers,
a lullaby, the lie of *live forever*
since no child yet has managed to step
over the body's million trip-wire tragedies.

7. *Presentation of Jesus at the temple*

I want to dwell on those who go unloved,
first Joseph, right hand in a money-purse,
left clutching a taper, which alone among
the others stands unlit, its wick dangling limp.
His gaze parses the tiles; he's a man
trying to decipher some meaning in his life.
Above the baby's head hang marble scenes
of violence: a sword, an axe carved white.
Two bronze boys support the altar, naked
as the baby, not much older. How can

anyone bear their labor, even as picture?
As though the point was always to divide
heaven's fruits along luck's unequal lines,
when it's written: every single child is God's image.

CALLING THE NAME

You do not appear
To be listening

To the syllables
That spell

Who you are, though once we used
These to charm you

Out from your forest—wild
Hoofed one

We turned into kin.
You won't remember that night

Your father and I shouted for hours
Until you, drenched, gasping,

Climbed out
And flopped finally down

On this berth where every night now
You revolve, forming the hands

On a clock that tells only
One time: how old

Through devising you
We have grown.

PLANS FOR THE NEXT ICE AGE

Imagine: no more whiskey-
Sipping while smoking black
Nat Shermans from a balustrade

Listening to Depeche Mode
On cassette tape; no more sequins
For skater skirts at the roller rink.

We'll have just a couple of flints,
Some funky mushroom soup
That makes you see stars,

If you're lucky, on the limestone walls
Plus fucking to pass the time—
They always had that in spades,

Plenty of dildoes and flutes,
Pretty jewels too
Fashioned from cave

Bear bones
And red paint.
Ochre on the tits.

Well, *plus ça change*,
It's all coming back.
Waters will rise, then fall,

Dragonflies the size of kites flitting over,
Viruses making a prison break
Out of the mass-grave sites

From Buchenwald to Wounded Knee.
Gentlemen, ladies,
Let's take the show

From the top—we'll run through
The whole act once more,
This time without champagne.

AT THE STOP & SHOP

Who are these gents and misses,
Anonymous, I live with
In the abyss,

Listlessly drifting—
Shopping cart before horse—
Through aisles of frozen veg?

Some appear to have been
Excavated from chalky soil
With a rake that strafed them,

Some are shiny with money
And minerals and leather,
Avocado oil, precious metals,

But everyone has eggs in their eyes
Sausage in their mien
Handwritten lists

From invisible kitchens
Where they feed from the trough
On Grandma's famous recipes...

Nobody here has the strength to lift
A spear or aim a slingshot to take down,
In concert, the mastodon in a meadow:

All the mastodons are dead, anyway.
Instead, I've hunted out and found
A jar of hot honey

Denatured tomatoes
A new charcoal toothpaste
That will reduce my teeth to a tabula rasa

So that whoever peeks in my jaw
In some distant millennium
Won't recoil from my stains in the dirt

PROVISION

For a long time I fed the children
From that inexhaustible larder
Money offers

But with the stores depleted
It now appears there's only one well
Here that never runs dry,

Just one bulb in this house
That never goes out
Even in the hoarse, bluish

Hour when dawn spreads
Toward the horizon's
Bald patch of trees,

When my earliest chorister
Leaps in the crib
And begins her orisons

Reaching out for this flawed
And dotted coastline
On which she'll press her lips

To drink not milk
But time through a dark
Nipple.

GIAMBATTISTA VICO

Oh Giambattista, I ask you,
What is the point?
Like you I try to write

In a house brimmed
With squalling children
And dinner-stink

(Only difference is
I also made/clean these...)
Brilliance resides in the mind

As a sliver of diamond
Jammed into the brain's folds
Slits a secret passageway toward God.

—No, I'm busy on Saturday, sorry
Chess lessons
Storytime

Playdate
I bring home the bacon
Then make it with pancakes

WEARING THE PURPLE

Here is my robe of office,
My robe of state
A sweatshirt and well-worn pair
Of jeans from A.P.C.,

My diadem
An unkempt ponytail
Of half-brushed hair;
No juice of the sea snail

Do I wear, no mucus
Of the murex dyes
My daily raiment a Tyrian shade,
Nor do I wield

Scepter or orb,
Unblessed by pontiff
Or holy oil nonetheless
I'm no less

Imperial in my demesne,
Two sets of stairs
And a mess of rooms
Where through a curious reversal

Of fortune it's my dependents
Upon whom I wait,
Even now in soft
Beds the kids lie curled asleep,

Dreaming, maybe, of that day
When through a fate
Inexorable as tides
They'll push me

Finally from the empress's
Seat—
Or stance, really, here at a sink
Up to my elbows

In suds and dinner grease.

SIREN

The alarm rings
You've forgotten
Something essential

Like your medication
Property tax bill
That black lace dress

Last worn in '93
You'd meant to dry-clean
And put on once more,

No longer seventeen—
Back then, you checked the boxes
Showed up early

To your SATs, "Achievements."
You did so well on the LSAT
Your mother won't let you forget it.

They were handing out golden tickets
That day you walked the other way—
No filthy lucre for you!

On a bank of the Ganga
You donned saffron robes
Said you were a poet

Reading Eliot in the light
Of a hostel's bare bulb
To a circle of interested bugs...

And now the siren rings
And sings from the nightstand, incandescent
With meaning

As though to say, THIS
IS THE LIFE YOU'VE CHOSEN
YOU WON'T GET ANY OTHER

PRIVATE PROPERTY

The rain was rough
The ice was worse
The hundred-and-fifty-

Year-old slate tiles
Have started giving me
The side-eye

I'm new to this, home ownership
I wash the wood floors
And make beds with fresh sheets

I walk down the street
Passing, like a stranger, by
Though secretly I know

This is my house, my dirt
Where the grapes are beginning to stir
With their ideas of the future

The way a poem stirs
In an alphabet,
Where already desire and nostalgia

Are starting to spin
Tight webs about the books and sleds
That belong in my kids' toy chests

So that one day when someone asks
What do you remember of your childhood home?
Gently they will smile, thinking

Of the place where their mother
Screamed at them
To pick up their shit

KILLING MOTHS

A crushing quality—
Rosegold
Velvet residue,

The iridescent wings
And shadow-making
Thorax in the end

All soft inside,
So soft its body's almost
A form of water,

A poisonous spit.
And where are the eggs
You want to know,

Where is the desire
For sex and dream of flight
On this stained wall?

You want to see between
The beads of that curtain
Which screens the door

Separating living from dead,
Between the atoms to whatever
Thread held this flimsy fabric

Together in one piece
Till, with a tissue,
You unraveled it

Even though you too
Will be so loosened
One day soon.

A DAY IN MARCH

The day is a drudge
A festering
An affect of mind
You crawl up on the beach
Thirty years
To say the same thing
Disheartened
Coming apart
Is the same
You've got this inclination
What is it lady moths
Up on my walls
Out of the chrysalis
Perhaps a year?
Of instinct that leads
So the object of desire might
The ladies leave their eggs and
A broken wing
Declension of the light
A dry sublime
Barely breathing
You've been trying
You don't want to get
But you're slowly
A day on Mars
As here, only redder
In the head or chest—
Feel when they crawl
And hang there, waiting,
Having fed on expectation
O radiant light
One through the dark tunnel
Surprise on entering—helpless,
Then what's left?

SMALL TALK ABOUT WEATHER

You're my friend, Sun,
So I'm sorry
If you get bored of us

Telling stories about you
That can't possibly be true:
Chariots in the sky, sea serpents,

Pyramids thirsty for blood.
They make us feel
We can touch you

Though you're the one
Who's forever reaching
Us with your rays...

Not today, though.
Today is comically ugly
Like a hagfish

Riding sea scum,
A gray that chokes, this cover
Of clouds that loudly shout

FUCK YOU.
Oh March, no one
Can even say

You mean well.
You're mean
Deep in your bones.

L'HALLALI

At the trumpet trill
All the walls
Fall, a seam opens,

The doe
Sprays a sort of final
Writing over the snow

As the world goes on
Shutting its door.
Happy birthday.

Everyone in this painting
Wanders wistful beneath a lofted
Whip, true master of the scene,

While the dogs, who have traveled
Such a long way for the money shot, go
Absolutely wild

THE EIGHTEENTH CENTURY

Seeing them in their foppish wigs, you wonder
        what were they thinking? But they bled too
with their bayonets, hunting accidents,
        stillborn babies. That was so long ago
they believed in humors then, saw dragons
        in dinosaur bones. Though what do you know,
anyway, who today told your five-your-old
        the computer can somehow see a clock,
who spins fairytales of viruses and vitamins
        you read about on a website somewhere?
You have no proof of anything. Your only data
        is years spent here, though every decade
the view changes. The wheel turns.
        A night janitor washes the blackboard blank
but not clean, not truly: there's a smudge.
        A trace of what happened.
In the portraits, they're beribboned, powdered,
        posed against a backdrop of cloud,
hollow-eyed, hugging pampered spaniels:
        they're paint, an image, a meniscus on what is
like that film of oil upon the ocean
        a speedboat leaves in its wake.

TWELVE VARIATIONS ON ETCHINGS BY GOYA

A deficiency of listening, or
These eruptions are a form of witness.

*

You're in the well you always
Had been, shouting for help that doesn't hear.

*

Shadows and grays. A darkness
That ticks, is filled with something animate.

*

Evil is intelligent and intimate. Soft
As a pet, with sparkling fur and eyes.

*

Intimate as though you wished it. As
Though you cooked it in a pot and ate.

*

That's what a nightmare is—something
More than entering. It becomes you.

*

Monsters are written into the earth, the hills,
Landscape. But it takes man to see them there.

*

I saw it. I was the man. Bolted all day
From Marathon. I alone am returned to tell you.

*

What's worse—the automaton or a thing
With wishes? Reason or the dream?

*

A broom, a bridge. A bride with a fringe
Of withered skin. Ugly angels with tarnished wings.

*

Mask and wig, triple-flounced dress. In the cave
Of faces you take a fresh one, grow new.

*

Specks of dust chatter amid feathers, while
A sky looks down on them, alight with fixed stars.

ANDROMEDA

The story has it wrong. All by myself
I clambered down that rock and slipped my arms
Inside the iron cuffs, just for a game.

The first hour was spectacular. Night-birds
Passing overhead like streamers unraveling—
After a while it grew boring, though, the ocean

Falling back in skirts of lacy foam, the stars
Walking a drunken moon back to her room.
Then only the distant blowing of a whale

Spouting his fantastic fountain charmed me.
If I shouted, my voice splintered, returned
Settling echoes at my heels like dogs.

I didn't mind. I was growing clearer
The way a pond clears after a mammoth explosion.
Pinned at the wrist and heels, I blossomed forth,

A spinnaker attached to some good mast,
So vast I swore I made the whole planet move
Until they arrived: not the monster,

It was harmless, I mean that shadow with the sword
On the shadow with wings, I mean that one
Who wanted to steal my fame from me, and did.

THE BOOK OF JUDITH

For fifteen years I waited to be needed;
Ladies, hush. You have no idea what
It is to save yourself like precious acid.
Fifteen years of sackcloth, pasting my face with ash
And sitting by the river watching visions,
Heads floating downstream in baskets like shorn
Marigolds nodding loose of bloody stalks.

Always I knew I was a pen-knife, a key,
Was bits of lapis lazuli fallen
From some lost statue's eyes—I *must* have a use.
And so I listened in the wind's whistle
For that spectral bell, that gold-throated
Messenger gathering me with his scythe
In from vespertine fields.

Then how sweetly I came near the general
Sinuously circling, a jeweled cobra
Lapping at his neck with my forked tongue.
Not even when I lay my body down
In the marriage bed, offering its plot of rich soil,
Did I sway and hiss so deliciously, gazing in
The mirror of his face as our eyes grew huge.

WHAT A SURPRISE

I rule the skies,
The weather, the drought,
I made this snowed-

Under afternoon—
Don't hate me.
I'm not raving.

We all need a piece of ice
Sometime, a sliver
Right in the kisser

Or gizzard, a blessing
Of frost dusted over
Soft eyelids.

Consider it
A preparation
For riding into that long

Rime-edged sleep
Under the hill,
Turning to crystals

In secret, like diamonds
Made from the bones
Of parakeets.

Cold shows us
How to be slow
Until we're as slow

As stone, silent as the iron
Face of the mirror
On this afternoon, or any other.

THE SPANISH FLU

Women with fever sigh in their sleep,
sleep that restores them to the state of sea,
they push their sheets off like an overcoat.
Outside, in the hospital yard, grackles
begin to complain amid the tuberose,
a train uses the track's ruler to bisect the view.
In the women's dreams: gowns of crinoline
and velour, phonographs and chilled champagne.
They're eating plums with lips that become fruit,
then swing around the dance hall's carousel.

THE WAKE

Slowly wearing a groove into the wooden floor,
They circle the body laid out on its gurney:
First the snow leopard, in its cloak of Argos eyes,
Then the tigers, leaps squeezed into their lean thighs,
Last the lions—debonair, tails flickering,
Their mountainous faces draped with impassivity.

But her body has turned off all listening.
Far astronaut, she has found another galaxy
And shut the communication systems, so she can float
Into the bosom of distance without talk.
They can have her mouth and tongue
If those old friends want, they can even have this heart

Whose orchard anyway is poisoned and never
Again will bear fruit.

ANGKOR WAT

I heard you calling at the gate:
You were gray and green, your fingers long.
You crooked one skinny pinkie,
And the night rolled on.

The night roiled into a silver furnace;
Night oozed like a well.
Things got pretty indeterminate.
I don't recall the words of this spell.

I've lost the trail to where time began
But I know that it ends in a field.
It ends with thousands of stone people
Whom the wind will one day unpeel.

The future has a past with lichens and moss,
Nutcrackers, rusted cannons, and beer;
The past is a place where the moon dips
Her face and tries her hardest not to sneer.

Between these points like a gondola lift
Time shuttles back and forth the whole day.
A passenger, I stare, terrified, down
At the rocks where we'll stop when it breaks.

LITTLE VOICE

You say I'm not alone
When I'm alone

When I point out *This doesn't feel right*
This isn't our map

You lie right to my face
From inside it

And for this I thank you
Yes, I appreciate

And have even come
To rely upon your lies—

Now I need you the way the stone
At a grave needs those lilies

That upon it, out of anonymous pity,
Some passerby has laid

IS IT ALL RIGHT

Is it all right to have a wish   to have
a perforation   to require a thing

must I wear my long black lace veil
like a lady from the nineteenth century

who can't show anyone what she's made of:
from underneath she must have seen   the world

in spots   as though afflicted   by syphilis
is it all right if I tell you my true name

which won't be found on any paperwork
if I light a candle in my brain

once two lions patrolled my perimeter
while a king cobra fanned its hood out

over me for protection   you see
what they knew was   I was suffering

my benefactors, I never needed
to hide from them my mind   someday I'll go

live in caves alone I won't ask anymore
for permissions will build a tremendous

fire prance alongside covered in blood
by its light I'll be smiling

COSMOS

I sign my name on the contract anew
Every morning that I walk to school.
Pulling a little kid in each fist,
I pay the future for those bodies we borrowed.

I prepare for my replacement
By filling their mouths with the whole jar of marbles:
English words and mincing syntax,
Dates, the names of revolutionary men.

Soon they will become the is and I a was.
At best, I will be a late-Roman shield
Thrown in a bog, engraved with illegible prayers,
Or a murk-dirtied corpse like a burnt candle,

Pollen-dusted rings moving concentrically
Away from me. Look at those two
Crossing the street, radiant with new day,
More beautiful than I have ever been.

Listen: I'm not sad. As long as I can,
I will work my little flute, which is to say
This body with all of its stops
Making a sort of music.

FOSSIL

I lived in the time of God.
We formed a net.
Together we hardened into jewel.

CHILDHOOD

I was born in another country
I don't belong to anybody
I fight for an army of one
I stare directly at the sun

I rampage through dirt
Scorch leaves scramble up trees
Make friends with the first
Crocuses of the season

Learn from them the secrets of death
Cast spells using rocks and seedlings
High up in a saddle of the tallest
Cedar I've fallen asleep

Tears dried on my cheeks
I speak my own language
Can write it out in new runes
Already I am waiting for poetry to save me

AT THE PRICE CHOPPER

Such pretty apples in their crate
All suspiciously clean—
They're integers on a balance sheet.

They're pure ideas
Straight from the brain
Of Monsanto. No Eve

Or Adam, no worm ever nibbled
On the likes of these Granny Smith.
Somebody in a lab somewhere

Must have mixed the chromosomal
Brew from which they grew
Till the day a robot picker

Strafed their orchard's leaves
With metal fingers:
Et voilà, aisle three, behold

The apple sanitized as a baby
Doll who only feigns
Her pee and weeping.

It's a cyborg—half-malic,
Half-plastic. A fantasy of nature
Without the dirt, the maggots,

Without death. But
Despite the best efforts
Of capital and machines,

Death is with us, us real ones.
Animal, vegetable.
The rot leaks out,

Spreading its stain like the black mold
Parading over this produce
Section's popcorn ceiling tiles,

A sort of Alexander leading his army
Through the Gedrosian
Desert perpetually. It's on the move,

Always coming for me, like that man
At Hampi, 112 degrees when he stuck
His face grinning into mine

As though he had my death
In his back pocket like a bright idea,
Or that crevasse-cut field where I tiptoed

On my skis through the bleak,
One way or another, coming for me,
And it's all right.

Whoever talks to me
About headstones, I say
I prefer sky burial,

Leave me outside for vultures
And the like, to the extent permissible
By Health and Human Services guidelines.

Not for me some mahogany
Sarcophagus or that waxy cast
Slathered on by the beautician

At the funeral home
Where they made my father
Look like a Pez dispenser

Who ran out of Pez
Laid down on a satin pillow
And hence to the pretense

Of sleep. I'll take the sky
Any day, the mud
Sweeter than whatever

These apples on their Styrofoam
Tray ever tasted
In that God-forsaken factory

Where they were shaped.
An American apple, wrote Rilke,
Is empty and indifferent,

A pretend thing,
A dummy of life.
I'd rather try my luck

With a bruise, take flesh
Softly mush-spotted
As an old woman's thigh

Between my lips—feeding me
By filling my cells
With its memories of summer breeze.

After all, I prefer myself
Bat-winged or dewlapped,
Crow-footed or smile-lined,

To some confection that refuses decay.
This way it's plain to see
I've had my years

I lived here

I HAVE FOUND IT

The sun comes up anew
        like a collision.

It's the day of the emergency,
        the accident.

It's the date of a happening,
        just like every other.

Out of her mother
        a baby slides

into rude light and receives a name.
        Then nurses bring

the stamp pad and apply one tiny
        ink-slathered foot

to a sort of contract. Everything has
        to be perfectly legal

for the bequest of this
        battered planet,

this sweetly belabored thing—
          one November night

I too once opened my eyes
          to the bright

NOTES

Duino Elegies is in dialogue with the ten *Duino Elegies* written by Rainer Maria Rilke, which he composed in part while staying at Duino Castle near Trieste, put at his disposal by the Princess Maria von Thurn und Taxis, the castle's owner and his patron. The embroidery known as the Bayeux Tapestry immortalizes major players of the Norman Conquest.

The poem "Lucky Girl" makes reference to "The Love Song of J. Alfred Prufrock" by T.S. Eliot and "Climbing Everest" by Frederick Seidel.

Giambattista Vico was an 18th century Italian philosopher. His autobiography, further elaborated upon and embellished by the Marquis of Villarosa, bemoans the burdens placed upon the professor by financial and domestic obligations, which hampered the progress of his work.

"Life of Mary" is in dialogue with seven oil-on-oak panels painted by the Meister of the Marien-Leben (Master of the Life of Mary), six of which are held in the Alte Pinakothek in Munich.

L'Hallali is in dialogue with Gustave Courbet's painting "L'Hallali du cerf." "L'Hallali" refers to a huntsman's bugle call to action, which is similar to halloo, both etymologically derived from *hallelujah*, itself derived from the Sumerian war cry "E-el-lu-lil-lum."

"Twelve Variations on Etchings by Goya" is in dialogue with Francisco Goya's macabre and visionary *Los Caprichos* (*The Caprices*) series of black and white etchings.

"At the Price Chopper" refers to a letter by Rainer Maria Rilke, in which he laments: "Even for our grandparents a 'house,' a 'well,' a tower they were long accustomed to, yes, their very clothes, their coat, were infinitely more, infinitely more familiar: almost everything a receptacle in which they found the human and added to the store of the human. Now, from America, empty indifferent things are forcing their way over here, sham things, dummies of life...A house, in the American sense, an American apple or a vine there, has nothing in common with the house, the fruit, the grape into which went the hope and contemplation of our forefathers...Living things, things we lived which are conscious of us, are draining away and can no longer be replaced. We are perhaps the last still to have known such things." (To Witold von Hulewicz, November 13, 1925)

ACKNOWLEDGMENTS

Grateful acknowledgment is made to the editors of the following magazines and journals, where many of these poems first appeared: *American Poetry Review*, *Fence*, *The New England Review*, *The New Yorker*, and *The New Republic*. Thanks, too, to the Academy of American Poets' Poem-A-Day project. Grateful acknowledgment is also made to the editors of the following anthologies: *The Penguin Book of Indian Poets* (Penguin India), *A World out of Reach: Dispatches from Life Under Lockdown* (Yale University Press), *A Century of Poetry in the New Yorker* (Penguin Random House).

I am thankful to Yaddo for the gift of time.

Thank you also to everyone at Four Way Books, particularly Ryan Murphy and Martha Rhodes.

Thank you to Paulina Olowska for the use of her brilliant art.

Finally, deep gratitude to Michael Dumanis, not only for assistance with this book but also for sharing and co-creating the kind of poetry-making life I always wished for. *The Future* is for Julian Dumanis and Leela Dumanis.

ABOUT THE AUTHOR

Monica Ferrell is the author of a novel and three books of poetry, including *You Darling Thing* (2018), a finalist for the Kingsley Tufts Poetry Award and the Believer Book Award in Poetry, and *Beasts for the Chase* (2008), winner of the Kathryn A. Morton Prize and finalist for the Asian American Writers Workshop Prize in Poetry. Born in New Delhi, she lives in Vermont.

Four Way Books is grateful to those individuals who participated in our Build a Book Program. They are:

Anonymous (10), Robert Abrams, Debra Allbery, Maggie Anderson, Kathy Aponick, Sally Ball, Jean Ball, Victor Basta, Adria Bernardi, Richard Blanchard, Laurel Blossom, adam b. bohannon, Lee Briccetti, Anthony Cappo, Anne Babson Carter, Cyrus Cassells, Jennifer Christman, Peter Coyote, Kwame Dawes, Michael Anna de Armas, Brian Komei Dempster, Patrick Donnelly, Lynn Emanuel, Joan Frank, Rigoberto González, Rachel Eliza Griffiths, Catherine Grossman, Naomi Guttman and Jonathan Mead, Beth Harrison, Jeffrey Harrison, KT Herr, Carlie Hoffman, Melissa Hotchkiss, Thomas and Autumn Howard, Parker Howe Foundation, Catherine Hoyser, Linda Susan Jackson, Elizabeth Jackson, Liz Janik, Marilyn Johnson, Deborah and Maria Jonas-Walsh, Elizabeth J. Kandall, Maeve Kinkead, Lindsay and John Landes, David Lee and Jamila Trindle, Rodney Terich Leonard, Howard Levy, Owen Lewis and Susan Ennis, Ralph and Mary Ann Lowen, Maja Lukic, Ricardo Alberto Maldonado, Donna Masini, Cleopatra Mathis, Lupe Mendez, Dale Neal, Mary Jane Nealon, Kathy Nelson, Marilyn Nelson, Nicole Nevadunsky, Kimberly Nunes, Rebecca and Daniel Okrent, Cathy McArthur Palermo, Marcia Pelletiere, Megan Pinto, Martha Rhodes, Paula Rhodes, Laurie Rosenblatt, Lyris Schonholz, Soraya Shalforoosh, Jennifer Skeele, Mary Slechta, Page Hill Starzinger, Sarah Stone, Yerra Sugarman, Marjorie and Lew Tesser, Reed Turchi, Maria Walsh, Martha Webster and Robert Fuentes, Calvin Wei, George Whalen Jr., Mark Wunderlich, Kathleen Zimmerman, and Carol Zoref.